I AM NOT A PIONEER

poems by Adam Fell

H_NGM_N BKS
www.h-ngm-n.com

FIRST H_NGM_N EDITION, MAY 2011

ISBN 978-0-9832215-2-4

Cover photograph by Suzi Crase
Book and cover design by Scott O'Connor

The inferno of the living is not something that will be; if there is one, it is already here, the inferno where we live every day, that we form by being together.

-Italo Calvino

What makes you think I'm enjoying being led to the flood?

-The National

CONTENTS:

11 Information Accumulated From Interviews of a Random Sampling of 1000 American Citizens Between the Ages of 18 and 65

One:

15 Reckoner
19 Limbo
20 Universal Healthcare
21 A Poem for Emily
22 From an Unattributed Source
23 Friend Poem
24 Looking Through a Tall Fence Toward the Ballistics Pond
25 Surplus
26 A Man Who Does Not Want to Be Identified Nor Explain His Situation Sits Down
29 Thylacine
30 There Must Be Something Left of the Minotaur in Me
32 Friend Poem
34 Yellow 6 Lake

Two:

43 For Suzi, April 6th
46 Balance
47 Lake Effect
49 Bomb-Making Materials, Pt. 1
50 While Searching the Internet for Nude Photographs of Women Who Look Like My Ex
51 Transmissions from the Satellite Heart
53 Preservation
54 In Absentia
56 A Young Technology
57 Bomb-Making Materials, Pt. 2
58 Human Resources

Three:

63 Slow Dance Slower
66 One Child
67 Making Light Echoes
68 Near an Empty Fountain in the Food Court
69 While the Committee On Television Discusses Whether Non-
      Residents Under Age 65 Should Be Able to Hunt with Crossbows
70 Ten Keys to Being a Champion On and Off the Field
81 At Acadia National Park, the Morning of Peter Jennings' Death
82 Makeshift Memorial
85 Coffin Tree

Acknowledgements & Notes

I AM NOT A PIONEER

INFORMATION ACCUMULATED FROM INTERVIEWS
OF A RANDOM SAMPLING OF 1000 AMERICAN CITIZENS
BETWEEN THE AGES OF 18 AND 65

48%   wait quietly for their turn beneath the median trees,
      watch the lowest branches abscise, watch fathers tow
      little storms across the yard.

38%   dive from the public pier, daring the still missing college
      girl to touch them, daring her hair to flow up and kelp
      weakly against their treading feet.

53%   keep telling themselves the unseasonable violence is not
      inside them, that their hearts are not flammable and filled
      with students hurling rocks at tanks, prying car doors off
      their hinges to shield themselves from riot police.

32%   remember that after the funeral their friend was asleep
      and all they could do was sit at the hotel window and stare
      at the construction of a bank.

57%   believe that, though their hearts and meat are flightless,
      a thin band of colorless light stretches from them to a place
      far above them where a child might be playing in the dark,
      but they are too small to see the place or the child or what
      is being played with in the dark.

29%   remember that, the day they learned the Battle of Franklin
      was fought beneath that muffler shop, that strip mall, they
      ate lunch around two; 9,000 dead, wounded, captured men:
      Midas, Alamo, Little Caesars, Gap.

34%   see that sheet of ice torn from the sidewalk and are stunned
      like a heron, waiting, waiting, for the stillness to catch up.

42%   believe there and here is only a beauty that resembles a small
      flashlight beam that does not diffuse in the atmosphere,
      a small flashlight beam that even a child in the dark can flick
      on and off on and off on and off.

Margin of Error: +/- 5%

11

RECKONER

Overnight, the lake invents itself.

We wake to the sudden beating
of its body against our properties.

The sudden beating. The sudden beating.

Neighborhood pets begin to disappear.
A child goes missing.

From our cars and homes we skip
rumors across its face.

Panic ripples.

We vote to close debate without debating.
We vote to gather our rifles and torches at shore.

We throw fire at the water, misfire,
throw fire at the water, misfire.

Our fingers ache in the tips
from matches burning down.

Our fingers calloused round and gripping
the handles of shovels, thousands of us,

filling the lake with beach sand, shore sod,
the expensive audio equipment
the wealthy use around here as wavebreaks.

We keep filling, keep dredging.

We dump parked cars in the lake.
We dump the parking meters.

We dump the bags of change
collected from the parking meters.

We dump the parking enforcement jeeps,
the leftover parking line paint.

We dump wooden-hulled boats,
paddle-wheel boats, boats stored
without lake since 1920.

We tear down the massive estates.
The massive estates go into the lake.

Mike says, why not the trees?

But the pine stands near shore
cling to the small piled sides
and soils of each other.

They are the first to offer defense.

Then we remember their quiet muscles
might be drawing lake water up to their boughs,
so we stay them put, we leave them be.

We read that somewhere.

But they're edging the cliffs, Phil says,
without the trees, the cliffs could landslide
into the lake, that would be a big help.

It's true we decide.

Into the lake the trees go.
Into the lake the cliffs go.

Into the lake the sun seems to go,
but we didn't throw that in,
didn't even think it.

Well, maybe we did, but only a second.
We know its just an illusion,

like the night taking the daylight
from the lake's face,

replacing it with its own emptiness,
which is really an illimitable fullness.

We read that somewhere.

Kyle has an idea: to keep the night to work,
we should install floodlights on shore.

He's right, we agree.

The floodlights peel open the iridescent grey
skin of the lake, the workers, the neighborhoods.

We fill and fill the night lake
until our muscles ache out of our shirts.

We're running out of things,
running, running, things, things,

but the lake still calmly takes
what little we give it.

It opens and swallows, opens and swallows.
Never a complaint.

Around midnight we run out of rubble.

We vote to create new rubble
of the little shops of our town:

the curio shop, the swimsuit shop, the fudge shop.

We make rubble of the library,
the Legion post, the banquet hall.

We vote to unbuckle our warm,
well-lit homes from their plots.

Our warm, well-lit homes go into the lake.

Bill says, I wonder if some of us shouldn't,
you know, throw ourselves in as a sacrifice
to the cause of wiping out this, you know, terror,
this sudden unknown destroying our...

Bill stops.

We know he's been awake all night
perfecting his speech in the mirror.

Bill stares silently
at his reflection in the water.

Because we separate
like ripples on a blank shore,
Reckoner, take me with you.

We think: where have we heard that before?
It means something vast to us.

We too stare at ourselves in the lake,
see our faces sequined with light to its surface.

We realize we go no deeper
than the top-first threadings of water.

So we volunteer to throw ourselves in.

We all volunteer to be martyrs.

But by morning
none of us have gone through with it.

LIMBO

Light falling on snow
is naturally cast upward,
but we are not designed
to fully contain the glow.
We wake in the dark of the woods
and must go forward.
When we are killed, we respawn
a few feet back until we solve
the error that wrecks us.
Each time, our bodies make
a sound like yielding,
a comprehension, a crumpling.
A burning barn glitched
behind a restless static of leaves.
Hatchlings on the beach at night
scuttling toward the city,
mistaking it for the horizon.
Devotion extends forward
despite our bodies' failures.
We leap and leap across
the voltaic rooftop letters
of a falling HOTEL sign.
We kill its current, watch it startle out.
We barely reach the ledge.
But *barely* is sufficient in a moving world.
Our flashlights make the cattle leak
from pens to pockets of drying grass.
To face ourselves, we respawn endlessly.
There are not fresh hoof marks.
There are fresh hoof marks.

UNIVERSAL HEALTHCARE

When white walls peel there is only lavender
and the snow outside killing things.

We sit in the yard, watch men take our house away
in handfuls,
                          watch the neighbors make a fort.

They watch us watch between slats,
pack their snowballs tight,
                    disarm the homes around us.

I see the small bones working in their wrists.
They see the small bones working in mine.

                    The sky has its carpals too
                              and a smaller way to yawn
                         without its mouth rearranging;

a white mouth blowing cold wind at us all,
untangling summer's aigrettes from our teeth.

We sweep more ash to the bin.
Take the bin to the curb.   Wait.

A POEM FOR EMILY

I don't know what to call a field
of black telephones ringing,
but I know what to call the terror
of a mouth that is wet
and maybe a hand on a breast.
I know that bravery is what's left of the body
when its organs are removed for donation
and the heart is drained and packed in ice
and is the tender pink of its homemade yearning
to produce blush after blush after blush.
You think me alone but I am only alone
when I watch you make ridiculous gestures
with your arms and legs and call it dancing.
When you call it that, I feel alone
because I call it the stealth assassination
of dignitaries about to break ground on land
designated for a new industrial park.
I call it the eavesdropping
and interrogation of suspected conspirators.
I call it the boarding of their water
and I call it the dogs.
I call it the hiding of this spring-loaded blade
in my robes, the clinging of me to the inlay
of the mosques and cathedrals and synagogues
that surround the ground about to be broken.
A field of black telephones ringing.
I wait to strike.
I wait for the golden shovel of the vice president
to prod at the pre-softened earth,
to uproot the first black telephone,
its body and cord, its frantic vocalization.
I wait because there is an arctic timing necessary
to building a giant mess with tiny tools.
I wait because I am alone
because you call this dancing.
I wait because I need information
but a field of black telephones ringing
only has a name once its gone.

FROM AN UNATTRIBUTED SOURCE

Ten more have died today,
while we sit here

punk
                    and drooling;

    gill-rakers
        dissolving our cartilage
in Pabst.

There's a crossbow on the wall,
its bolt drawn at the label-peelers,

     the boothed kids,
                            botched like us,

                                            decanted
                                                and chiral;

                empty cigarette machines,
                                                gutted,
                        knobless,

                a colony of new garbage bags,

                                lying in the parking lot,
                            unfurled and chirring.

    We leave our flasks as an offering,
    the alternatives are cureless.

FRIEND POEM

When you arrive on a bridge
suspended above a mighty jungle river,
fleeing from religious zealots that are a part
of a secret order of religious zealots,
I will be that bridge and crumple myself
and untwine the ancient twines of my ropes
and shake the ancient dust caked on those ropes
and halve myself as you just reach the safe side.
And the religious zealots will crumple with me
and flail with me and when we descend into the river
together, they will no longer be religious zealots
but condensed packages of nutrient-rich materials
that will flow to the sea and become food
for the living snow that drifts
through the baleen of enormous creatures,
feeding those creatures and keeping them
safe and happy and full
in the collected deepness of their bodies.
And the collected deepness of my body
will crash into the river below
and become wood and wood and vine and sisal
and I will be one again with the lands
I'd been made from and made to connect
but never needed to connect
and you will be exhausted and wipe the sweat
from your brow beneath the canopy
and weep for those poor religious zealots
and their families and the world
they would have murdered you for,
the flooding world that is the collected
deepness of all of our bodies.

LOOKING THROUGH A TALL FENCE TOWARD
THE BALLISTICS POND

Near second day, a herdless wind
grazes on wrecklings of dead corn.

It startles at my approach.

                    Its hooves unwisp the soil
              of the ammo plant,
                              surface the casings
              of long-ago cartridged men,

                    their fossils, un-planted
              and re-
                        near the concertina fence.

Two shots ache the bluffs around me.
I smell the carbon come
                         vast,   oleum-eyed,

                    through the halved skulls
              of the decommissioned buildings.

   I check the boxes:

              ☑   Yes.   I am aware of the lead.

              ☑   Yes.   I am aware of the DNT

                         cocked and clotting
                    the chambers
                              of each placid well.

   Near the highway, a man hauls
   two soft winds from the gravel.

          Their small hooves tip, slosh,
          fail slightly from the pick-up bed;

      the road venting its imperfections
      on their limp, entangled heads.

SURPLUS

They've left two tanks
in the parking lot of the old ammo plant.
Their barrels point across the highway
at the gas station and a subdivision
where a man welds beautiful things
from the wrecks of old machines.
On his front lawn, a tree-sized heart
being killed by a tree-sized arrow,
flocks of flightless birds
made from musical instruments.
There is no blood.
There is no music.
I take my sad leavening for lint,
play with its soft pieces in my pocket.

A MAN WHO DOES NOT WANT TO BE IDENTIFIED
NOR EXPLAIN HIS SITUATION SITS DOWN

❖

Near the turret grave of Julien Dubuque,
the soft bend of my arm gathers

the dark blue primer
of this first night's staggering on.

An empty Doritos bag uncrumples
itself against the sandstone.

Empty plastic bottles bright
inside with beads of condensation.

I hear the mass of fir and aspen
incessant behind me.

I hear the Mississippi still panning
its vein of deep earth below,

still piling torn strips of its own darkness
onto small patches of sand.

The kids alive here yesterday
called to a barge through the chicken wire,

threw small, futile rocks from the cliff.

Slit the waves of the river without meaning.
Slit the fanning, fanning wake.

Their laughter dove to skim the water
like swallows; young voices

now vague, mammoth,
mouth-sprayed white on cavern walls.

Something crucial just out of distance.

❖

In the parking lot, someone's left
their headlights on in the panic;

thick, white necks of light
tangled in the barbs of the fence,

ends hewn off by the dark of the the bluff's edge.

I confiscate all I can of what is left
inside my own frame, inside the crawl
of their clean light onto drainage.

White stars, cliff face, sandstone, plastic kiosk
molded with the story of Dubuque and the Meskwaki:

the Native-cut lead, the keelboats of pelt and ore,
the beautiful daughter of the chief.

The red lights of the cell tower across the river
flinch and blink out.

Wisconsin, emptied
of its old concussion of distance,

left with only the logic
of abandoned materials.

Silage heaped in flatbeds,
tissue scraped from cutting boards,
plaster silt from pounding nails.

The grafting of immediacy to fear.

I try to imagine there is still a Burlington
across the river, where my mother loves me,

helps children with learning disabilities,
researches our genealogy on the internet.

Have I always needed this clutching
at light to hoard a yield of myself?

27

❖

In the Mississippi River Museum,
there are five freshwater aquariums
and a replica of a protected wetland.

In the recreational area, people are buried
in a mound the shape of a heron.

I remember the discarded tanker truck
capsized in the woods near my parents' home;

its hide coralled with birdshit, rusted gutshot belly.

Birch bursting up through the dripping
of its tameless liquid paunch.

There is life still in the drainage of our skulls,
in our least love and cry and synapse.

Life still in even the retina's last feeding,
in the brain-green tufts of us

bursting up through the woodgrain,
the polymer, the metallic,

the charred dusk of us, dusted up,

clung in the trees, scattered
by the palings, the brush, the breeze,

into caved fields, gymnasiums, riverbeds,
the small clasps of lawn between pavement.

The brain-green tufts of us
bent at stalk, drying to hay to tinder.

Our bodies kindling our bodies,
lost with fire, sumptuous with fire.

THYLACINE

Somewhere in this delta there is a tape of me
imagining myself less a handler,

more a houseless yard matted beneath blankets.

When I leave, there is a brief pause.
The rain stops beneath the overpass.

What I mistake for silence is the sound
of everyone else shutting their windows at once.

THERE MUST BE SOMETHING LEFT
OF THE MINOTAUR IN ME

The children load me into the trailer,
padlock the tailgate, take the dirt road,
past the sanitation plant, the tannery,
the strip club where my friend
watched his student dance.
I put my arms through the grates,
feel dry wind, feel chaff and silt.
There is the long fence, there is the far complex.
I see the first fields maw, bristle-mouthed
wide with the wrecklings of cornstalks and soy.
I see the long, scuffed lines
of my friends being lead into buildings
by men with glowing sticks.
The workers greet the children,
unload me, laugh at their prodding,
at the glitch they make of my muscle beneath skin.
They tend me toward the line, toward
the funneling fence, the doorway.
I can hear the lowing of my friends around me.
I can hear the faint-dull puff of the bolt gun
at the temples of my friends already inside.
I can hear the collapsing, the skidding
of hooves on the draingrate, the hum
of the tangling machine lifting them to be slit.
I am nearing the doorway.
I am nearing the doorway.
A gray cloud catches in the sky
and our bronchia unrest, the men and mine,
and my friends ignore us.
The cloud stills, stalls the dry light,
brings the blunted shadow.
The men notice this.
They scuffle to look up at the sun,
bearable enough for their eyes to gather
into guarded piles for an instant.
I smell their eyes catch
like living motes in the light.

A uterine second of distrust.
This is the moment I needed.
I am not a pioneer,
I am just scared to my animal blood
of the doorway, of the men,
of what they will keep of me
and what will be grist.
I take my first step
and cannot untake it.
I gore my way through the men,
feel their stomachs give,
feel the razorwire,
the chainlink buckle before me.
I run.
The children scream near the trailer.
I run.
The gravel milling my hooves,
adding me quietly
to the dust by the teaspoon.

And you collapse near a horse cart full of hay
in a city known for its medicinal properties.
The cautious leaves of the city's trees fall only
on those who need to be touched.
Its rodents only drag their food off into deeper darkness
after they've made sure the starving are well fed.
But the bustling people filling the marketplace now
do not live in the city as you and I do not live in the city.
No one lives in the city because the city needs no one
to live in it. The city takes care of itself.

Every day people travel from the outskirts
of the kingdom to visit or work.
Some bring goods to set up in the marketplace.
Some take their place as the elders of the city,
some as the clergy, some take their place
as the president and congress of the city.
Others are the poor of the city, the children
laughing in rags or splendid gowns,
the armed forces at strategic points,
the merchants coaxing their wares into wage,
the protesters encircling the capitol.
All these people come each day to inhabit the city
because they need the city and the city feels obligated
to help all things it takes inside itself.
The city has designed its life to aid what must be aided
at the exact moment it most needs aiding.
If a person collapses, the lacquered walls of the city
stretch themselves and soften themselves to catch
the poor soul who, having collapsed, the city is plentiful for.
The city takes us in as its blood each morning,
and we gladly transfuse ourselves
because blood is both plentiful to us and scarce.

But when you collapsed in the recent past,
near the horse cart full of hay,
the city did not reach out its walls
nor its gate men, nor its presidium,

though the city did notice you
and longed to plush itself and cup itself
to catch you and heal the failing tissues of your body.
It yearned for contact with you, the contact you needed.
It cried into the cloths of its homes
because it could not keep you safe.
It wailed its anguish into signal fires in its guard towers
and the urgent torches of its first responders.
But the city had so many people to help this time
and it knew I was coming from its outskirts
and would be there in minutes to help you up
and walk you through the indescribable rushing
of people trying to help all the hundreds of others
that one man had killed himself
to make collapse all at the same time
on the street in the marketplace of the city.

YELLOW 6 LAKE

Quietly, it is the television
that frames us.

Safety no longer in numbers
but in the fog of our windshields,
the lowering of our blinds.

It's this safety I'm afraid of.

This pointless reloading.

This waiting for the water to come
and lend our blood its transparency.

Until then: a carload of sparrows

reading each morning to us
beneath our window,

and a room full of kids at school
who don't lose their leaves like we do,

who don't find their jarred blush
red enough to seal.

❖

Near Western,
in the streetshade of broken 40's

and the stalebreak laugh
of women pouring leche,

there is singing still.

There is singing still
in the rooms we have left.

There is singing still in our brothers.

It might be a metaphysical thing,
or an idealist thing,

or, maybe, it's just the way our bodies
barricade themselves.

❖

Though just September,
they've put the pumpkins up for sale.

We set the table with newspaper,
pull out the carving kits,

let the kids scoop out their pulpy hearts.

This business of being containers
for guts, or for candles,
for little birds that asphyxiate first,

leaves tender little to love in one's chest,

tender little to remind us:
the kids never see us take our guts,

so orange against our too-many-night carried frames,

back out to the fields each night
and re-plant them in rows.

❖

Speaking of distance
and speaking of sleep,

we've returned, softly,
time-and-a-halfed.

The tourist larvae have hammocked
between parking meters,

poised and gauding
each torn cusp of streetlight.

It's been years since we've seen them alive,

but we've been reading of legions

marching interstates,

forging spears and shields from Metra rails.

We hope you've come prepared.

This is our signal moment.

Things are getting political.

Please though, don't worry,

the manual we all pitched in for
is safehoused and soundbit.

We don't need to resort to page 473 just yet.

❖

At the podium:

It is true that we can only write
about rain so much

before people start to figure out
it is our own creation.

You are right that we are failing.

There is always someone leaving,
always a rhythm to the vacuum.

I see our glasses raised

but they all seem to leak
from the floors above.

The chandeliers catching
our regrets in their skirts.

One last time.

The sparrows are reading.

The legions are poised.

The children are outside
looking for crickets.

Here's to our home, my friends.

It is ours to re-tooth.

It is ours to fend with rain.

FOR SUZI, APRIL 6th

You can hear the dead I made
crowded nearly still in the street outside.

I know you can.

And I know how much it reminds you
of the soft wrestling of those life jackets
we saw floating on the lake without bodies.

I can hear them too.

I made them, so I know
they will wait endlessly.

I've been trying to write down this escape plan for us.
It's so well formed in my head.

And I've been trying to make you a care package
of rations I have left from the looting.

The important things I've taken
from stores and others' bodies.

I've filled a box with Band-Aids, bottled water,
a Campbell's Chicken and Stars.

I know you're skeptical.

No one for the mail in a week.
Power cut Friday.

But my body still hoards the smell of your skin
before saliva in its mouth as it breathes.

So I need to try and write this.

Thursday: I'll have the sniper rifle ready
on top of the bank across from your apartment.

You'll have to run as fast as you can.
I'll try to draw the dead I made
away from you with human noise,
as much as I can make.

I know they'll be listening.

This'll give you time. I hope.

God, I'm trying.

Remember, if they grab you, keep low,
I'll try to take their heads if you keep low.

And what is filling your chest as you read this
is a by-product of the guilt inside you,

the guilt that blames yourself for the failure of my body,
my mistaken body that is not infallible hero,

but an untrained, barricaded, secluded body,
a body just without aim in your distance.

And what I want you to know,
what I need you to know,

is that your guilt is more senseless than the dead
I hear now crushing themselves against the door.

It's the senselessness that's terrifying.

If you read this you'll understand.
If you get this package you'll understand.

God knows you're more a survivor than me.

You calmed me when I thought the wild horses
in Medora would trample us on our air mattress,

when I flinched at the wounded bleating of animal
that woke us in the dark of Itasca.

There is a grizzling of throats in the hall,
the clawing of shredded hands at the door.

There is a distance of shouts from the window.
A defacement of that distance, those shouts.

Human sounds, just there, alive, somewhere,

above the dead I made at the door,
above what might be birds

tearing through the down of their own bellies.

You will survive me.

You will survive me, I know.

Weight crush splinters frame.
The heavy, human rust of their breath.

I love you. Please,
don't make me look at their mouths.

BALANCE

I tear the styrofoam packaging of my new year
to pieces and make rickety angels in its drift.

What else is there to do?

Shame is a caucus of unblemished skulls
objectively critiquing the intentions of my mouth.

I've started a new entry for it in my portfolio
of grizzled, mid-western industries.

I note its uncommon talent for gristle,

the gray clot of human noise and grip
its made of my one true sledding hill.

No matter which atlas I buy,
the same bodies' remains.

The floral and faunal decals peeling
from the exposed rebar of this guilt

that doesn't erode like the clean community
of laundry and light I surround it with.

Don't know about you.

I've spent my winter filling the rooms of this house
with mobiles, ferns, the restorations of prairies.

You wouldn't believe what my heart smell like right now,

abraded of that glorious stench we cobbled together
while all around us the concerted fields of Wisconsin
were being classically trained to erode into sprawl,

that glorious stench of us

eating wild blueberries in the mountains,
destroying indestructible cars in the snow.

LAKE EFFECT

A.:

It's these guts that need a place to be,
these guts, collapsing, tugging out my skin,
tugging cradled, my outside, fumeless skin,
these guts that need a hand to heave to spine,
my tender shim, my skinny tender shim
of sky, the city flogged, my skinning hands,
my hands skim curdled light from spun-lake dark,
the faucet collapsing and collapsing,
the water's fault-cut bloom skinning my hand,
this gurgling inside me, cut, collapsing
onto stones; her water falls onto stones,
her water sutures my self, the sky here
contains her, my skin contains her, my guts,
their whir and murk and folded guilt, contain her.
I will not rise, as me, the lake is gone.

S.:

Icicles on the coal cars this morning.
Near the walk, clumps of walk pretend to dark.
The loons, cloaked with lake, scatter dagger-board.
The torn walk is leveled for me but slants
in snow. In snow, my dark prints contain me.
The white contains me and the lakeshore begs.
The white contains him. Bleach, window cleaner.
He poured from me, has left, the smell of night
in the cedar chest. The smell of him left
amongst my sheets, amongst the startled sheets.
I wash the rug. I wash the rug. The rug
flapped out, the rug disloyal and leaving.
The snow is light, it contains me, does not
contain him, but does contain him; the smell
of night and loons and fading cars destroyed
by distance, by sleep. I wash the basin.
The rug dries, contains him. The basin dries,
contains him. The rug and basin dry. He left me.
The snow is not white because men leave dark prints.

47

I contain white, the loons contain white, bleach
creates white, dark prints are contained by white.
He is contained by white. The dark prints left
mean we contain white and are contained, cars
brace the white as the city braces sky.
Seatbelts. Consummation. I am contained.

A.:

I tear a shim from the city and prop
up the sky, I tear a switch from the sky
and throttle the city, throttle its kind,
throttle the planks of its rootless siding,
I left her paling with snow beneath eaves,
I left and glistened as I left and cried,
I glistened without light, unmade of light,
driftless, dragging sutures, the lake is gone,
its snuffling waves are gone, the lake is gone
and now the barges, now the sumped barges
leak along the river, dislodge and lodge
the waves, the river waves, dislodge, Dubuque.
It's this guts that lodge and dislodge, barges
leak along salt-clopped steps, the road leaves
the red-shift clime of buildings, the barges,
the lock and dam further on, the river,
its broken legs caught beneath my engine
block, its curt thighs caught beneath my engine
block, I left her but the snow contains her,
my heart-scattered salt, sand-melt, plow-scrape, I'm breaking
this control, I cleave through the barges, the leave-strain, the state.
Inside me and outside me there is a glisten without light.
Inside me and outside me
there is a piling of moisture that will not last the day.
The conduit snaps shut
and the dusk-light contains her.
I contain her. She contains me.
I reach for her and we scatter slightly
into the dust and cush and phosphorescence.

Christ their necks, their stunned necks,
the cheerleaders, lush hair up, their lit-
wick throats, barest throats, collapsible
wicks, hands on mine, barest hands,
pulling my body up, up? yes, up,
scared up, from taserpoint & plasticuffs,
from boot-necked to the young bar floor,
the cheerleaders hold me, now, all, together,
above themselves, above the crowd,
above the riot cops, the shards of spit,
the brown glass spit, the gassing spit and eyes,
the choking kids, the townie kids
wrapping themselves in caution tape,
the college kids tipping over
the car euphorically torched,
their groped mouths groping mouths,
their Mag-lite eyes bursting with happiness,
a happiness like a barricade,
but at least, god, a happiness,
a makeshift shield of happiness,
their chapped lips smudged red
on the chipped glass rims of harder mouths.
They finger full the flames, they fist
and fling and flail their burning fists at me,
at me above them, high above them,
higher now, the cheerleaders raising me,
my bloodier threads, dripping already, already?
on the sidewalk, on the damp grass, on the parts
of the cheerleaders I will never be a part of,
the moving parts most stunning when they're still.

WHILE SEARCHING THE INTERNET FOR NUDE
PHOTOGRAPHS OF WOMEN WHO LOOK LIKE MY EX

In the glass of the city, I practice
my engine noise. I lob it at the windows,
the monitors, the business end
of an intersection's security camera.
I lob it at the door to the door of my home,
at the dog upstairs, always barking,
always rubbing his fog on the capitol's flanks.
I lob my noise at the front window,
its bright gape sweating, goggling
the street-tits. I lob it at the woman
on screen, eyebrows salved Etruscan
kiln-bred, fire suckling fire.
I pause at the cesarean scar.
A surveilled city grows uncontrollably
in the barren consequence of the moment.
There is a sound of yielding within me,
a comprehension, a buckling of girders.
The glass of the city reads me quietly
to itself: sawing, gristle, heart
tucked pornographic in back.
My groping brain decants from pane to pane,
windshield to windshield, shutter to shutter.
I blunt her into lens and leer and glut-light.
I halve her into halation, into slurred
refractions flung window to window,
my onlooker's eyes careening her
into crumpled frame, roll cage, puddled
primer, rubber, plastic, caustic smoke and fire.
Here is my hesitance to act before emergency.
Here is my hesitance to fund the inspection
of my own crumbling infrastructure.
A tragedy is so easy to create without hands.
One irretrievable, open-mouthed gust
and the rivets snap beneath the bottle-necked traffic
I call my kind but babeling heart.

TRANSMISSIONS FROM THE SATELLITE HEART

The innumerable men wait
in the stadium for her performance.

They swear into hush when it begins.

They surge in their seats, their saliva and tears
leak out into each other's aisles,

flooding the corporate boxes,
the concession stands, the mezzanine.

They clown at first, throw
their plastic cups of beer onto the field,

throw their garbage into each other's mouths.

They shake and collapse in the grandstand.

They stall and then flee and flee to the field
where she stands on a stage at the fifty yard line.

The men weep around her, breathing in piles,
reaching for her, trying to comfort their bodies

with hers, climbing each other
to discard her for her flesh and flesh and saliva,

the smell of her between her breasts,
between her earlobe and hairline.

There is the heavy breath from the loudspeaker.

There is the conformity of their spines
to what they believe is her spine.

They bend and unbend, brush one another.

They startle at each other's touch,
strike out blindly, caving each other's
chests and skins and fasteners

with torn-up bits of bleacher,
the disfigured hollows of stairwell cages.

She stands still on the stage above them.

She stands still as they scrape their trunks
in oblique, apostolic agony.

Her long skirt and its beckoning hem.
Her long skirt and its clutching to flaw at her hips.

She stands still on the stage
and ignores the men in their rapture.

She stands still on the stage
and stares above their creaking bodies.

She is waiting for something to happen.

She is crying but there is no door for her to close.

She is a biology teacher.

She knows the name for every thing in their bodies
cutting itself to make her love them.

PRESERVATION

Because of our bodies, we must,
of course, have a ventilation system.
Otherwise, the atmosphere inside us
becomes too stifling to store
our foragings, our longings and dusks,
amongst our already buckling shelves.
We give them quiet slits at certain angles.
We produce their sounds for them,
tender their closed spines with barest fingers.
In a technical sense, our living surplus
of failures is low-use material,
but the straddling lobes of our bodies,
their mouths and sex and burning glands,
welter against oxygen and catalogue,
against vast, windowless archival.
We wake startled each night by their babeling,
lamp ourselves frantic to sketch new designs
for the more patient species of lust
we work so feverishly on.
Attempt after attempt at transplant,
our bodies always rejecting
such lenient models of carnality.
If contrition is a reason for reconstruction,
it is not the act itself, not the minutiae.
Leave the sweat to bead the dancing girl's calves.
Ply our groped mouths from the groping mouths.
We control the temperature of our warehouses
until the temperature becomes what we store.
'We fight the collusion of our bodies
until our bodies complicate us possessively.
But does that complication *create* us?
Does its possession compel us
toward a more quarantinable lust?
A more absolute contrition?
A contrition so precise in its shelving
of all our bodies have foraged.
Our bodies so precise in their confusion.
Our bodies rejoicing yet abraded
as we make unbound brains of their longings,
as our unbound brains make hearts of themselves.

IN ABSENTIA

I began in this dawn wavering

like a baby goat's legs
on its first steeper ledge,

wavering like its tiny, trying muscles,

like damp tangled hairs
trickling over unchipped hooves.

Try it.

Waver. Tip.

Here is my body.
Hold me up to the light.

See the shadows of my known organs.
See the outlines of the unknown.

Hear the pumping, the gurgling, the acids.

Heavy, aren't I?
Heavier than you thought.

Why so surprised
considering what I have inside me?

Think of all a stadium holds,
even when it's empty.

And then count all the stadiums inside me.

Hold me up to this light.
How many do you see?

Its not easy to tear a stadium down.

See the dawn drip through the masses left,
brush the puzzled grass,
the corporate boxes, the loge level.

See it flush through each retractable dome
like wet tissue and semen ghosts in toilet water.

Great, now I'm seeing ghosts.

The world in this dawn has pin-burst and pierced me

like a lion's eyeshine caught mid-
kill by the headlights of a television crew.

Watch the red muzzles of their babies emerge.

Watch the gentle lapping.

Even killing machines have to lick their cubs clean.
Even men have to be emptied of their stadiums.

I creak and guzzle and yap in this light

like the empty molded seats, like the men gathering
drunk in parking lots, like the baby lions tearing.

They are all inside me.

They are all inside me, I know.

I try so hard to be careful.

A YOUNG TECHNOLOGY

There are so many high school girls here
but it is only their perception that seclusion dehumanizes
that I put into my mouth.

They say their car doors are stuck with ice
and, I assume, inside, they too
are filled with every kind of loneliness.

They don't know yet that makes us powerful.

I'd bless their hearts, but it's not that easy.

Their synthetics blushing in the fainted yard.

Their abundance paned
with this fragile winter breaking against itself.

BOMB-MAKING MATERIALS, Pt. 2

Downed, they let me, the cheerleaders,
the cheerleaders unhand me, all of me,
my fingers streak their beaded arms,
smudge their beaded calves,
their faces of powdered shell and sand,
turn away, they turn away
from me and seep and bank and settle,
they fade into doorways, into dorms,
into lofted beds and futons,
the highest step in the stairwell,
anywhere recoverable,
where no one can touch them.
They leave and wet the city's morning
as they leave and slur the lobes of me.
I am garbled, garbled but gallantly safe,
because of their kind bodies, their kind brains,
their footprints now just crushed grass, god,
my fuckt loyalty, my shivering, my snuffling brain,
my body, my body, the cheerleaders gone,
I know they're gone, but still, I feel
their blood-flush, pore-scrub,
I feel them through the cinderblocks,
the paint coats, I feel them on the one
soft cake of skin left beneath my arm,
the bruises of their fingertips yellowed
just to health, this health, thank god,
this health, thank god, their kind brains,
their kind bodies, thank god, even alone,
even asleep, even in sweats, they broadcast,
on a loop, even as they dissipate,
unconfirmed reports of a new world
forming around me violently
with one less intimacy of glass
to have never put my fist through,
one less tongue to have never let in my mouth.

HUMAN RESOURCES

Not quite sure what the dawn
keeps shoveling over us

but there's a pond full of it out back.

The ducks there have mass, give mass,
die slightly from the water.

In mass, they flee toward the porch
as a dog sets upon them from the path.

In the kitchen, I don't know why I'm nervous,
so I douse myself with green tea, makeover shows.

Bright veins open. Five beers in,

I imagine the windows of our home
unblown from glass to sandstone cliffs,

swallows looping our necks like sprung snares,
some lost goat refusing to climb.

I try to dance it out.

I tear the labels of the beer bottles to shreds.

I write a stick-it note to you,

press it to the TV screen:

Dear heart,

I'm sorry, but I am not a pioneer.
I'm just scared to my animal blood
of what will be kept of us and what will be grist.
If you come home, please, just let's sit with the pond,
let the dawn dissolve us in its gathering.
The anthropologists will be here soon enough.
Mistaking my semen stains for gypsum glyphs.
Ignoring the drop of your menstrual blood
I leave to share the gray, fitted sheet of my bed.
Our preservation is not about us.
Our bodies are not our bodies poured from plaster.
I've left my heart and mouth and penis preserved
for you in ziplock containers in the freezer.

xo

-a.

SLOW DANCE SLOWER

We sit still together
on the darkest smokebreak bench

and do not touch.

We smell the burning of our own
particulate hearts in the air.

Smell the pine of them, the charred
last throats of our grasses

brushing for first against each other
as tentative wanders of smoke.

Devotion extends forward
despite our bodies' failures.

But our devotion, our devotion
is a doused thing of crumbling glow,

its human insides camouflaged
by our blackout city's quieting coals.

❖

Our bodies can't destroy everyone.

Flatness, green hills, industrial jobcenters.

Near the darkest smokebreak bench,
we unfake our blood,

reach out to each other,

illegible, cinder-glown,
post-traumatically quiet.

Together, our kindled lives mint new.

Roses spill into the parking lot,
nuzzling sport utility vehicles.

The industrialpark ducks rile and resettle
the shore-sod with their waddling.

Near the darkest smokebreak bench,
we slow dance slower

so the motion detectors can't find us,
so their wildless lights can't glitch us apart

like gull-plucked strips
of surfaced mother whale and calf.

Devotion extends forward
despite everyone's failure.

The closed circuits chir and chir
from the dark of the corrugation

but can not ashame us of ourselves.

We are coughing but alive.

We undark the dark of each other.

Our blackout city lungs
devoted in this moment

to our breathing,
to our breathing

in this moment

as one.

ONE CHILD

One second, the blackout city in my lungs
startles again skeletal with light,
one second, bronchia upon bronchia,
unpetaled branches upon branches,
I float all at once together
on the stream beneath the flower bridge.
one second, I'm breathlessly thrilled
with consumption, purebreds,
a new museum for each of our bodies'
sciences, one second, I am filled
with my own inhospitable brightness,
one second, I am blaring chemical redness,
each pipeleak blending into river,
blending with the cattle drinking the river,
the girls washing their clothes in the river,
giggling songs of moral good the older women
teach them at the eco-museum,
one second, I replace my shoulder blades
with the upswept roofs of the village,
one second, I replace tendon and joint
with rubber tubing draped upland from the well
to the ruined homes near the wind farm,
one second, I replace my mouth and lungs
with the white-masked women, bright blue
in the mechanism, molding Christmas trees,
one second, I replace my eyes with clouds
seeded with silver iodide, one second,
I replace my heart with the boy,
naked except for helmet, riding his new bike,
one second, I realize I love you as I nod off,
one second, I let the quilt slip from my chilled legs
into the fire, one second, I love you so much
I take the village with me when I'm consumed.

MAKING LIGHT ECHOES

My brother wades to me,   drunk eyes treading
light echoes in the mist of the hot springs.

He lends his eyes to cover the naked
girls, their hard,   dark   pits,   the chipped masonry
collecting the water into three torn mouths
each mending warmer than the next.

We watch the sublimation of the girls
into dark, drunken steam,   the re-beading
of their dim-pored bodies onto stairs.   Snow
pocking the coarse tile of their groutless backs.

Though hand-razed, this water has mortared us,
has lent our shared blood its transparency.

I create small waves with my hands,   float
an empty beer can across the water between us.

NEAR AN EMPTY FOUNTAIN IN THE FOOD COURT

The high school girls ignore the young
iridescence of their grackle necks
to grasp at snips of walled light
cast from their own sequined shrugs.
They flock past me to unbead
the dew from small piles of camisoles,
pluck scraps of baby-doll, low-rise, halter,
from the limbs of autumn displays.
In the store glass, they are collectors.
In the store glass, they are collected
into the sitting cusp of my reflection.
The lattice bench, the escalator, the fakest palm.
Pushing past the register, they push through me.
They shear in the glass, past me,
and puddle inside, behind me
at the tables of the food court.
Like the long-wet neaths of my arms
they collect the table's curled perspirations
of diluted bleach, the wisped white
larvae of a few shedding rags.
My cellular heart glows open.
Above me, sparrows
make their nests in the skylights.
And to somewhere I imagine ingrown
with mirrors, restlessly copsed
with tank-lace fringe and concealer,
I lose the girls, their darting
iridescence shed and left to puddle
black on the floors of changing rooms
as they try on brighter dresses.

WHILE THE COMMITTEE ON TELEVISION DISCUSSES WHETHER NONRESIDENTS UNDER AGE 65 SHOULD BE ABLE TO HUNT WITH CROSSBOWS

The windowframe has internalized the window,

has internalized the graceful scuffle of our faces,
our polite bodies crudely rigged
to crackle only against others as warm with contrition.

But this is not the time to be feeling for the glass
or envying its ability to break in case of emergency.

I have a stack of my students' lonelinesses left to grade
and can only manage the grammar, the spelling,

scribble in green ink that our value
is in what shelter we choose to go out from
bodily into an optional wilderness.

I tell them it might end up ok, who knows,
mention something about percentages.

Though the winter has recently begun to shatter
concentrically when lashed out at, maybe
its best to just keep watching the rabbit in the front yard,

something has to happen

besides the tempered pane of the world
jarring as the larger trucks drive past.

My students don't buy it.

They're good kids.

Hopefully, I tell them, no matter what happens
there will be someone whose job it is
to bring our newly fallen bodies back inside

like glasses of last melting
snow to the freezer.

TEN KEYS TO BEING A CHAMPION
ON AND OFF THE FIELD

1.

As far as I can tell,
            this all started
      at a Comfort Inn in Bemidji.

And all the beeps you hear while reading this

                        mean something
                              you can't just click
                        and drag to the trash.

   Thus far, the paths that leave here
   have been reduced to a key
   in the lower-right corner of the summer.

   That ★ represents us.

   That → where we may or may not be headed.

It's just started to rain

and I've been thinking a lot
about those two ducks we always see together,

                        and how I wish,
                  right now,

                              we were them.

2.

What we have here
　　　　　is a summer
　　that transcribes our President's speeches
into beds of seaweed
　　　　　shaped like maps of the world.

　　And what I need to do right now
　　　　　　　　　　　　to reduce their shear
　　　　　is lost on me.

As a result,
　　　　　I am feeling a bit Cahokian.

　　And I say this only because there is always
　　light on the waves:

　　　　　　　　　believe we are not cast
　　　　　　　　　in type,　　but rather
　　　　　　　　　printed in currents,

　　　　　　　　　if,　　in fact,

　　　　　　　　　the currents are still
　　　　　　　　　in print.

3.

By now, I've memorized where all the raindrops land
and have translated their surnames into 114 different languages,
classifying their origins into three distinct genealogical groups:

a) Gut-shot
b) Bridge-fed
c) Sifted

Today, when I was bored,

I began weaving a hammock
from the flight paths of swallows

and some willow fronds
I scarfed from the lake.

4.

Thing is:

        it's finally stopped raining here

    but all that matters right now
    are these waves
              canceling the hull.

    Today,
          the lake is freshly stocked

       with tourists,
                sprawl-raised,
                aquarium-eyed.

      They've mouth-bred
      and choked the water.

    I can walk across the deepest part
    but there's nothing Jesus about it;

    the shear breaking us

up

                into plates.

5.

I have nothing left to do here
but assume
there is something about you
in the way the aspens flinch.

Or   are those birch?

I should really be able to tell by now
and what that means to someone,

perhaps me,

is that I should try a little harder
to clean the stress

150 miles puts on an envelope
of little white flowers

and a Heineken coaster
scrawled with the meaning
of a dream I had.

If you haven't figured it out yet, this is my attempt at a semi-
annual beauty special. You will find a quiz on the following page and
it may tell you what you need to do in order to make yourself feel
better this season.

Or, maybe,   it won't,

and all this
is my attempt

at reprogramming
the tour boat's circuit

into waking up
to piss together

outside our tent
in the middle of the night.

6.

1. Though you are progressing satisfactorily toward a positive self-image:

   (A) You wobble like a tornado siren through the rolls of quarters, the spit-up girls, the paunch of sapless men toasting.

   (B) Your vitals glow scattered in the parking lot like the guts of crushed lightning bugs.

   (C) You believe in a pliable world, believe you are the pliers.

2. Making scenes in public places takes attention away from:

   (A) The citronella clouds, the water-spot stars.

   (B) Prop-struck, the college girl, still a month missing.

   (C) When we first met, a bison's head hung above the bar's register, our faces awake so late at night in its eyes.

3. At the risk of sounding mountainous:

   (A) The use of real blood was to be phased out over the course of the year, but the funding failed to be found.

   (B) Lately, you've come to an understanding of what it means to be both missing and missed, both the hand and its holder.

   (C) You've reached the point where nothing more can grow.

4. You are certain there is something more to this:

    (A) Near a spilt birch, your step-dad has augered a hole in the lake ice.

    (B) Its dark eyelet unbends to darken in white.

    (C) We take our hearts out and chill them in the same water to survive.

7.

I'm still hung-over
from two nights ago;

        the lake is beautiful,

but I've started to forget
some things cannot be bought

       or forced to migrate,

        even by thousands of tourists.

Right now, our caste
is typed
        at the aft deck bar,

   and,   unfortunately,

this is not just some corner
we've been backed into

      but something decidedly
           more de-veined

     and water-
         striding.

Our time being:
       we nestle
     together
         to the bottoms
       of the tourist's hulls.

     We hold our sprung-snare tongues.

     We allow our tip jar hearts
just defrayal enough.

As long as our waves are cursive,
our lines will never still.

8.

If you could see my path,
perhaps, even pick it up fresh
from the wake left behind,
you would see six circles:

> arrow plains with Clovis points
> sparring with the shore,
> labeled in cuneiform,
> never returning to their source.

The fact is:
> some paths cannot be cleared
> by our teething machines,
>
> only light strokes from each other,
>
> or campfire,
>
> leaving expressways to follow
> paths deer have worn panoramic.

I guess,   in a way,

I am trying to tell you
there are no answers here,

except,   for some reason,

I think a hammock between two trees
is what we should be shooting for.

9.

Yellow is health in campfire. Two babies looking at each other. Hands bloodless, graceful. With no wind to touch, the lake home windows re-cast me fulfilled, sustained, drained, dredged, developed.

In the coffee shop, a little girl watches me through the back slats of a chair. Her dark brown curls wind down her hand to the stuffed wolf she holds close by its throat. Her fingers leave small, dark prints in the white fur.

10.

This morning we walked to the lake
                    and built geoglyphs
            from shattered piers cribs

    and the fossils
    of multi-million dollar estates
built in 1906.

                We tied our hammock there,
                        between two aspens,

        with the bowline
                of our drowned tour boat

                    and the strand of deer path
            we followed to the mouth of Itasca.

Even as our shores recede,
we've got our colors out,

                paint on our hands,

        slurring the lawns
    of the lake homes

                    reckoner blue,
                    amoxicillin pink.

    We take axes to their adirondack chairs.

        We tag their effortless windows
        with our effervescent names.

The moon pulls each wave to us
and taxes can never be taken out of that.

AT ACADIA NATIONAL PARK, THE MORNING
OF PETER JENNINGS' DEATH

Near the sea wall, there is a picnic table
and two kids wrestling on the breaker.
They are healing together.
They are sealed in plaster,
signed by friends with different color pens.
One is an ocean I'd never seen,
wild blueberries, gulls
picking dead crabs apart.
The other, the sun playing Wrestlemania
in the hallway of two mountains,
spilling over the toy wrestling ring,
splitting both bones in its right forearm.
The tide is out; the intake nurse
is made of tiny water droplets.
She clings to the sun,   clouds it
with white blouse,   gauze,
lightly-powdered latex gloves.
By the time I reach the sea wall
she has lifted, leaving two unlit x-rays
on the windshield of a Toyota Corolla.
The sun is sitting on paper.
A chart tells me it is younger than I thought,
tells me experts in the field
no longer consider me a planet.
There is a painting of a deer near the ocean.
There is a separate heaven for medical waste.
I sit in a lawn chair on the rocks of the breaker.
Behind us, the waves practice their D'Nealian
on the gray water of the Atlantic.
There are two blue shores they touch
and a row of red buoys
that guide them near the middle.
Their penmanship is beautiful.
It will be a month before the sun can write again.
I smile and we shake left hands.
I can't help stepping
on some of the snails in the tide pool.
There are so many of them.

MAKESHIFT MEMORIAL

The truck is finally warming up.
More than rain has turned to snow.

With my window down, flecks of neighborhood.

Unlit homes and homes lit cold with cable,
the bolting of startled formations.

Between houses, I watch kids crush empty beer cans
between their boots and the frozen lake.

No one else here to notice them,
to notice the stoplight changing

so I idle and read the kids quietly to myself.

The radio clips the Secretary of State
into men blurting loose about terror, adaptation,
the protesters encircling the capitol.

There is a jarring in their voices,
something crucial just out of distance,

A feedback loop of untucked mouths.

Theirs is a safety I'm afraid of.
A safety no longer in numbers.

I haven't given up yet.

The boys beg the girls to chew tobacco.
The girls beg the boys to pull their sleds back up the hill.

They do not notice the junta'd lights across the lake
slogging the white air toward us.

❖

Near shore, the kids unfold in trace amounts.
Some passed out, some bleating.

Some filling condoms with spigot water, laughing
at the crude pocks of creamlight stalled in rubber.

On Dairy Queen napkins, I write these words

and these words sketch lightly a creaking nostalgia
upon the backs of the kids with my eyes.

I crumple each try as I finish,
glut the cab floor, the clotted dash.

There is barely a fiction to find of myself

in their clinging near the fire, their groping
to the shit-rum'd hearts of each other.

But *barely* is sufficient in a moving world.

It is all I can do to keep from burring softly
to the hems of their coats, reminding them

that the lake is never still below the ice,

that the trills of the blue jays stalling outside
are really the forward sirens of an untucked city,

a city fucking un-awed, a city dividing by dividing.

I want to get out. I want to walk to them.
Through the smell of new telephone poles.

Through the burning aspartame.

Through the slopping, citied snow,
the plow-heaps like massive smoker's lungs.

I want to summit and descent toward the fire pit,
the kids sleeping like kindling, covetless,
snow gauzing them unshaken and gray.

I want to have a blanket for each of them.
I want to take their soiled clothes away in bags,

hose the driveways clean of vomit, spilt cereal,
the long, dry skins of their sweet hearts scabbing over.

I want to make sure they're tucked in,
not leaving, not dreaming
of birds trapped behind heaters,

not mistaking themselves for vended litter
gathering in gusts against alley walls.

Walls they could regain with ease.
Walls they could kudzu over.

They think the cans they've crushed on the ice
will shhh into the lake once its surface thaws.

They think they are pioneers,

think they know what will be left
of them and what will be grist.

But I haven't given up yet.

I want to volunteer myself as a witness.

I want to fill out a form that says I am responsible.

I want to bless their hearts,
but it's not that easy.

COFFIN TREE

Somewhere in the national forest,
there is a coffin tree for each of us,
chosen at birth, containing us
completely, even in its youngest seedling.
If we keep no one left to love, to love us,
to cut it down and afford it carved
to order, we will wander the flower bridge,
the light-rail route, the geopark trails,
unclean ghosts the clouded blue
of our deepening cataracts.
What's left of us, children moved to city,
smudged air of our once bodies,
is holding, exhausted, the village
brinkline of trees from the road.
We disappear as the mist that beads
our shapes burns off at dawn.
There is a difference between fire
shaped like a horse and a horse made of fire.

ACKNOWLEDGEMENTS & NOTES

Without the hearts/brains/love/friendship of the following people, this book would not have been possible: Larry, Susan, & Tyler Fell; Suzi Crase; Caryl Pagel; Daniel Khalastchi; Ben Kopel; Emily Pettit; Michelle Taransky; Mark Leidner; Kevin Gonzalez; Lauren Shapiro; Nate & Thea Brown; Barrett Edward Swanson; Ryan Walsh; Katarina Riesing; Sara Jane Stoner; Jill Haberkern; Matt Hart; Nate Pritts; Srikanth Reddy; Brenda Hillman; and Dean Young.

Many thanks to the editors of following publications who first published some of these poems, sometimes in different forms and/or with different names: *Tin House*; *Crazyhorse; Diagram*; *Forklift, Ohio; Fou; notnostrums; Sixth Finch*; *Ink Node;* and *H_NGM_N*

A number of poems included were published as the chapbook *Ten Keys to Being a Champion On and Off the Field*, published by H_NGM_N Books. Thank you!

❖

The title "Reckoner" is taken from the Radiohead song of the same name and a portion of its lyrics are italicized in the poem.

"A Poem for Emily" was inspired by Emily Pettit's poem "Red Wings Collapsing".

"There Must Be Something Left of the Minotaur in Me" is a reworked segment of the poem "Dichotomous Key for Selected Families of Adults" published in *Tin House*.

"Transmissions from the Satellite Heart" owes its title to The Flaming Lips' album of the same name.

"Bomb-Making Materials Pts. 1 & 2" were inspired by The National song "Mr. November".

may 22 ███
4:03pm

dear ███,

      at the center of a mountain is more mountain, like
at the center of ourselves is more of ourselves, maybe a
bit riddled, porous, volcanic, but still even the empty
spaces are us, the molten rock is us. the immense
pressures. we can see a road there, through the center of
the mountain, can create it with our teething machines,
take the mountain away truckload by truckload. but then
what? an easier drive? is that all we were looking for? so
many places we can never get to without destroying, the
body, the outer reaches, without hollow-pointing our
arrogance through gutpackt spaces. we think we can never
really understand it til we get at its guts. but then its
gone. we're good at that, though. experts.

      i know we have very different environments these
days but soon we'll crash into the mountainsidetogether.
literally! I better get a salami sandwich while I can.
while we're indestructible. as our loved ones. as our
brothers. things are better with ██████. or at least,
the friend thing seems to be █████. I think glaciation
might be good for me. we'll see.
██
██
██
██
██
████████████████████████████████ I'm not planning on
telling anyone else, so keep it close to the nest ok? ███
██
██

      spaight street was a rotting, mud-lush thoroughfare
this morning. there should have been horses and meat-
cleavers and antler-hockers and wagons full of supplies
from Cheyenne. maybe a gambler lying facedown in the muck.
the men in orange vests, winching gutturals from the
leveling machines, do not belong here! i know they're
recreating the road and that's lovely of them, but i want
more gold-panning in the gutters! i want more calamity
jane! slept til 9am for the first time in a couple weeks.
through their hammers and metronomic clamorings of reverse.
beep beep beep. the clouds have been on my side lately but
couldn't get their shit together today. like me, they seem
to have issues with joining groups. by now, spaight's a dry
bed, sun-stuck, flat blue, fat blue jay crying, always the

whiners. though skins, swoops, snares so pretty as they're
sprung.

        speaking of shitheel thoroughfares and *Deadwood* and
Calamity, I keep thinking what Jane says to Joanie in the
first episode of the third season: *Each day takes learning
all over again how to fucking live.*

        i have nothing really to say about that. just wanted
it here, for our record. its enough to just sit staggered
for a moment. that's all I really want. the briefest flash
of awe. like a tornado snapping power lines.

        speaking of tornadoes, me and ▮▮▮▮ closed down The
Crystal the other nite and one of the bartenders, the gruff
one with the hat, had just smoked and then punched this guy
in a red hat out for flirting with his friend, flat on his
ass, flat brained, glass-smashed and ▮▮▮▮ held Gruff
back and sent him off home? in his car. everyone was
smashed on their stools. then the cops came. 5 cars. of
course. Guy-in-Red-Hat had regained himself, yelling at the
bartenders. i was on his side until then. he hadn't done
anything really to deserve to get punched, but Saint Amand
is the only saint I believe in. bartenders, the messless
surrounded by such meticulous mess. at least last nite,
whiskey-deep. so Red-Hat is now officially a shithead
forever ever after. since I'll never see him again. it was
rawk us.

        i'm actually about to go with ▮▮▮▮ and meet ▮▮▮▮
and ▮▮▮▮ and ▮▮▮▮ and ▮▮▮▮ at Genna's for happy hour. I
need a beer. spent yesterday shopping for mountain-climbing
gear. boots, rain pants, other stuff needed. breathable
mesh! aquamira! I'm getting really flustered and
gratuitously charged for our trip. soon. we will meet at
the edge of the mountain. wearing our sweaters like the
pelts of dead muppets. until then:

be safe and safe and safe. we need each other.

a.

Adam Fell was born and raised in Burlington, Wisconsin, and holds degrees from the University of Wisconsin-Madison and the Iowa Writers' Workshop. He lives in Madison, Wisconsin where he teaches at Edgewood College.

Photo credit - Amanda Manteufel